FLY-FISHING CALIFORNIA'S

NORTH YUBA RIVER

ED KLINGELHOFER

With Illustrations By

ROBERT ELSE

The Salmo Press

Publishing History

First published March 1993. Net proceeds from all sales of this book are being turned over to the Douglas A. Michell Memorial Scholarship Award at California State University, Sacramento, 6000 J Street, Sacramento, California 95819, where the authors and Doug were colleagues for many years.

Copyright © 1993 by Ed Klingelhofer and Robert Else.

All rights reserved. No part of this publication may be reproduced, stored in a retrieval system, or transmitted in any form or by any means, electronic, mechanical, photocopying, recording, or otherwise, without the prior written permission of the publisher. Printed in the United States of America.

Published by The Salmo Press
P.O. Box 329
North San Juan, California 95960

ISBN 0-9635201-0-5

This book is dedicated to the memory of

Douglas A. Michell

Friend, Colleague, and Fisherman

January, 1993

E.L.K.

R.E.

ACKNOWLEDGMENTS

This book has been cheered on by a legion of friends and supporters. We are immensely grateful to all of them. We are especially indebted to Ralph Talbert whose computer know-how made it possible to translate the brush-and-ink sketches which illuminate the book into reproducible form. Our deepest thanks also go to Anne and Pat Fleuret whose financial help made the book's publication possible, to Eric Gershwin and Nikki Phipps who gave us help with the preparation of the final copy, and to David Comstock whose editorial suggestions and advice vastly improved both the appearance and the content of the final product.

E.L.K.
R.E.

CONTENTS

Acknowledgments iv
Fishing Waters of the North Yuba vi

    Preface 1
    Getting There 3
    Gearing Up 4
    Highway 49 Bridge to Goodyear's Bar 7
    Goodyear's Bar to Downieville 11
    About Downieville 15
    The Downie River 19
    Pauley Creek 23
    Lavezzola Creek 29
    Downieville to Ladies Canyon Creek 35
    Ladies Canyon Creek to Sierra City 39
    Sierra City to Bassetts 43
    Haypress and Milton Creeks 47
    Bassetts to the Headwaters 49
    Salmon and Butcher Ranch Creeks
        and the Lakes Basin 53
    Hazards 56
    Useful Fly Patterns 58
    Campgrounds, Camping Areas,
        and Day use Sites 61
    Lodgings and Restaurants 62
    About Miners 64
    Incredible Free Offer 65

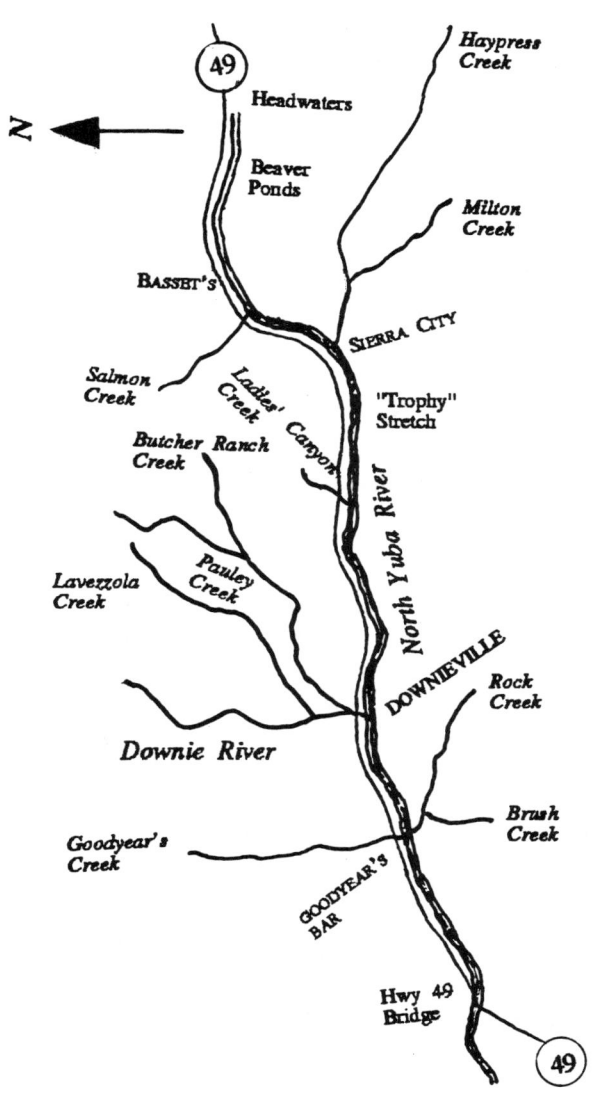

Fishing Waters on the North Yuba River and Its Tributaries

PREFACE

Sierra County in Northern California claims approximately 40 miles of the Yuba River's North Fork. Those 40 miles--from Cut Eye Foster's Bar at the county's western boundary to the river's headwaters atop the Yuba Pass--offer some of the consistently best fly-fishing in California.

In addition to the main river, its principal tributaries--Salmon, Haypress, Ladies Canyon, Butcher Ranch, Pauley, Lavezzola, Downie, Goodyear, and Rock creeks--provide exciting action. Taken as a whole the system teems with fish. California Department of Fish and Game censuses have counted 700 trout per mile in the entire main river, over 1,000 in the reach east of Downieville, and in excess of 4,000 in some of the feeder streams.

Not only are there trout to be taken--it is easy to get to. The river itself, closely paralleled by California's Scenic Highway 49, is never much more than a few hundred yards from the highway. Indeed, much of the time the river is right there at the very edge of the road. There are plenty of places to get to the water without undue physical stress and walking in the streams themselves is comparatively easy and safe. It is, in many respects, the ideal venue for older fly-fisherpersons. Those of us in our sixties and seventies can fish it comfortably and it is a fine, minimally hazardous place to pass on the lore and mystique of fly-fishing to children or grandchildren.

In this book we've tried to tell you and show you what the waters look like, how to reach them, what flies to use and when to use them, where to stay and to dine, and what to expect in the way of dangers and discomforts and how to avoid or minimize them.

The map on the facing page tells something about how the book is arranged. After some introductory formalities the next 12 "chapters" provide brief descriptions of the various parts of the watershed, telling how to find them, what to expect when you get there, how to fish them (or, at least, how we fish them.) Maps showing access points accompany. After the fishing information you'll find additional material--hazards to watch out for, lists of eating places, motels, campgrounds, patterns and dressings of useful flies, a bit on mining and miners, and so on. We hope that you find it informative and entertaining.

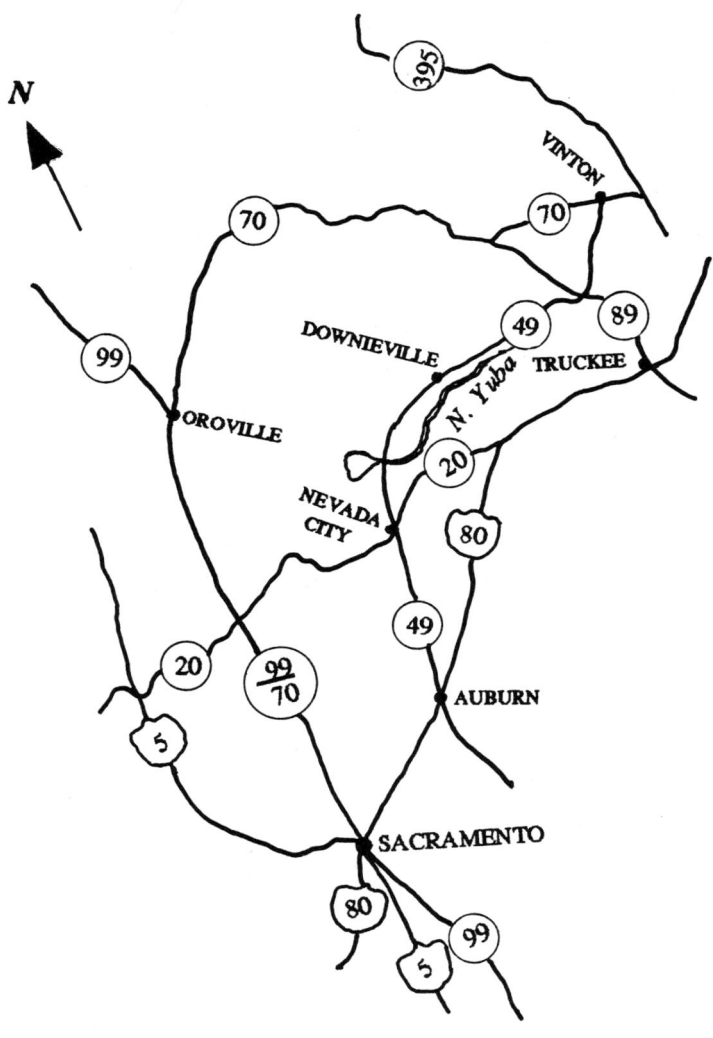

Routes to the North Yuba

GETTING THERE

California State Highway 49, the scenic Motherlode Highway, parallels all but a bit of the North Yuba River's Sierra County stretch.

If you're approaching from the west (Sacramento, San Francisco Bay area) take I-80 east to Auburn, 30 miles east of Sacramento. The second Auburn exit puts you on Highway 49. Follow the signs to Grass Valley and Nevada City and, at the eastern edge of Nevada City make a left, still on Highway 49, to Downieville. (If you miss the turn you'll be on Highway 20 headed toward I-80 and Truckee.) In succession you'll hit the Yuba River's South Fork bridge, North San Juan, the Middle Fork bridge, Camptonville, and eventually the North Fork bridge 3.7 miles after entering Sierra County. From that point the river and the road are never far apart.

After Nevada City the terrain changes, the open, rolling land giving way to steeper, craggier, more forbidding hills. Residences become few and scattered and the terrain is heavily forested. In the spring you'll see redbud, ceanothus, and white dogwood in bloom at roadside, along with California poppy, purple lupine, and, clinging to the sere roadside cuts, orange monkey flowers. The pines that line the steep North Yuba canyon remind one of nothing so much as closely overlapping fish scales.

If you're coming from the south via I-5 or U.S. 99, pick up I-80 at Sacramento and proceed as above. If time isn't a factor you can elect to go Hwy 49 much of the way by following Hwy 41 east out of Fresno or 141 out of Merced. They both join 49. Scenic 49 is a good 2-lane road; though it is slower it is more interesting because it respects the contours of the land and bisects instead of bypassing the worth-visiting little mining towns en route--San Andreas, Columbia, Mokelumne Hill, Jackson, Placerville, Coloma (where James Marshall spied gold in John Sutter's mill race and triggered the Gold Rush of 1849.)

From the north follow I-5 or U.S. 99 to Sacramento and I-80 or angle east where these main routes intersect Hwy 20. Follow 20 to Marysville and then to Grass Valley where 20 joins Hwy 49 briefly.

From due east, take I-80 to Truckee, Hwy 89 north to Sattley where it meets Hwy 49, then west on 49 over the Yuba Pass to the fishing ground.

From the northeast U.S. 70 eventually intersects Hwy 49 a few miles before 70 dead-ends in U.S. 395, the main north-south artery on the eastern slope of the Sierra Nevada.

GEARING UP

Except during the period of heavy spring run-off, the North Yuba and its tributaries are relatively easy to fish. The water will be crystal-clear (unless you're downstream from a dredge) and moving brightly through a series of deep holes, pools, riffles, and chutes. The bottom will be rocky and the footing can be treacherous, especially late in the season when moss coats the rocks in some stretches.

What you will wear depends pretty much on your tolerance for cold. Save for the early spring (opening day to mid-May) I usually go out in felt-soled wading shoes, heavy socks, shorts, long-sleeved shirt, billed cap, and polarized sun glasses. (My friend, Bob, who supplied the marvelous brush-and-ink sketches for the book, dislikes cold water intensely so he uses felt-soled hip waders.)

I carry and use a wading staff that attaches to the back of the fishing vest with an elastic cord so that I can sling it out of the way while casting without having to watch it float off downstream. Otherwise I keep the paraphenalia to a minimum--a modest fishing vest with nipper and leader straightener, fly dressings (floatant and...sinkant?), leader case, spools of tippet material, extra reel spool, insect repellant, sun blocker, and, of course, fly case. I like the Orvis flat leather shearling-lined "book" with zipper closure.

What equipment you use is entirely a matter of taste. I'm addicted to an old cane rod with an equally venerable Hardy reel holding #5 double-tapered floating (or floating with a sinking tip) line. I find the double taper is better for roll-casting and the terrain demands a good deal of that. The leader tippet (I use a tapered 9-foot leader) I prefer is a 7X. I use small flies, size 16 or smaller, either barbless or with the barb mashed down. I'll have more to say about useful fly patterns later.

Bob uses a custom Sage graphite rod that throws a #4 line; another friend, Jerry, also likes graphite with a #5 line while Jon, a true son, works with an ancient South Bend cane rod that takes a #7 line. We all catch fish.

Bob and Jerry also carry wading staffs; Jerry and Jon use wading shoes. Jerry and I usually manage at least one spill per outing so I keep my billfold above the waterline in a button-down shirt pocket. Jerry takes a hair-dryer to his wallet when he gets home.

It's easy to go to extremes when outfitting yourself. When fly-fishing I hold with the maxim that less is more. I'm out there to enjoy myself, not to bring a satisfied grin to Eddie Bauer's face.

Going to Extremes

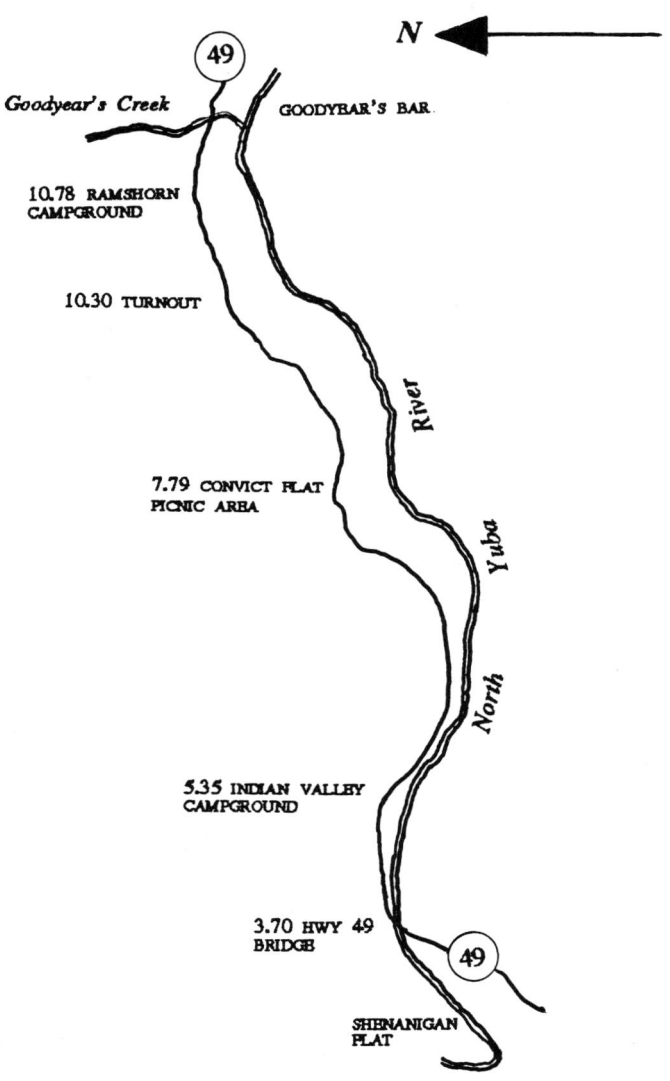

The North Yuba: Hwy 49 Bridge to Goodyear's Bar

HIGHWAY 49 BRIDGE TO GOODYEAR'S BAR

In case you haven't already noticed, Caltrans, the California state department that looks after the highways, has a system. At every point where something is likely to need tending they put down a metal stake with a mileage designation attached to it. For instance, the Highway 49 bridge over the North Fork of the Yuba is identified as 3.70 which means that the bridge is 3.70 miles from the western edge of Sierra County. We've used these handy markers to identify various points of access to the North Yuba from Highway 49.

3.70--HIGHWAY 49 BRIDGE

Immediately upstream from the bridge the river is wide, shallow, and fast-flowing. It bends north to pass under the bridge, narrowing to a chute just before the bridge. Then it widens into a succession of slower riffles and pools. Access is very easy. The road is just a few feet above the river with parking areas on both sides of the road at the eastern end of the bridge. I've taken fish (small plants mostly) from the pools immediately below the bridge but this particular stretch has never been red-hot for me. Useful flies have been Buzz Hackle and Ladybug,

SHENANIGAN FLAT

To get to Shenanigan Flat, park at the bridge, get your gear together, and hoof it west. Bypass the locked pole gate and follow the road that clings to the north side of the gorge. Shenanigan Flat used to be a Forest Service campground but has been closed for years. The road is in good condition and the one-mile walk is pleasant. Hit the water at the Flat. The water is good, riffles, chutes, and pools up- or downstream. I usually fish here late in the season and have done well at the edges of the current at the head of pools. Action slows markedly when the air and water temperatures are cold. Buzz Hackle and Pheasant Tail nymph have produced.

5.35--INDIAN VALLEY CAMPGROUND

This stretch is open and brush-free and offers a variety of waters. There are deep pools at Indian Valley Campground and near Fiddle Creek Campground downstream. Upstream there are a succession of riffles and slacker pools. The terrain is boulder-strewn but fairly easy to walk. There are usually some gold-panners around, working on suntans, blisters, and dreams of sudden wealth. Park outside the Campground entrance and make the short, level walk to the river. Then it's either up- or downstream. If downstream, begin at the lovely pool directly opposite the campground, then try the long, slow-moving channel until it flattens out into a broad riffle. At that point, ford the stream and work the chute and pool that eventuate near Fiddle Creek. Upstream from the Campground there is an interesting succession of pools, chutes and riffles. The pools at Indian Valley and Fiddle Creek hold larger fish; Fall '91 I took and released 15-inch 'bows on successive casts at Fiddle Creek. In 1988 I landed a 22-inch doe bursting with roe. She was the last fish I kept. The shallower waters upstream have been productive on occasion. particularly in late fall, mostly plants responding to wet flies and nymphs. Buzz Hackle accounts for all the larger fish; Pheasant Tail nymph, Woolly Bugger, and Gray Hackle Yellow have also worked.

7.79--CONVICT FLAT PICNIC AREA

Park at the Convict Flat picnic area and pick up the path to the river at the western edge of the entrance from the highway. The walk to the river is pleasant, shady, not too steep nor long. Lots of boulders at streamside; popular spot for gold panners. There are the customary chutes, riffles, and pools along here. The waters are attractive and inviting but I've never done well in this stretch and what luck I've had has been with an Elk Hair Caddis.

10.30--TURNOUT

This wide, flat site at the side of the highway is almost a replica of the Convict Flat scene without the picnic tables or the privy. During the season a large party of dredgers camp out in the parking area. The waters here are much like those around Convict Flat.

10.78--RAMSHORN CAMPGROUND

The campground is on the north side of the highway. To access the river, park at the day-use area on the south side of the highway and walk through to the river. There is good fly-water up- and downstream from the entry point but it is heavily fished in summer. Buzz Hackle has been effective along here.

The Highway 49 Bridge Over the North Yuba

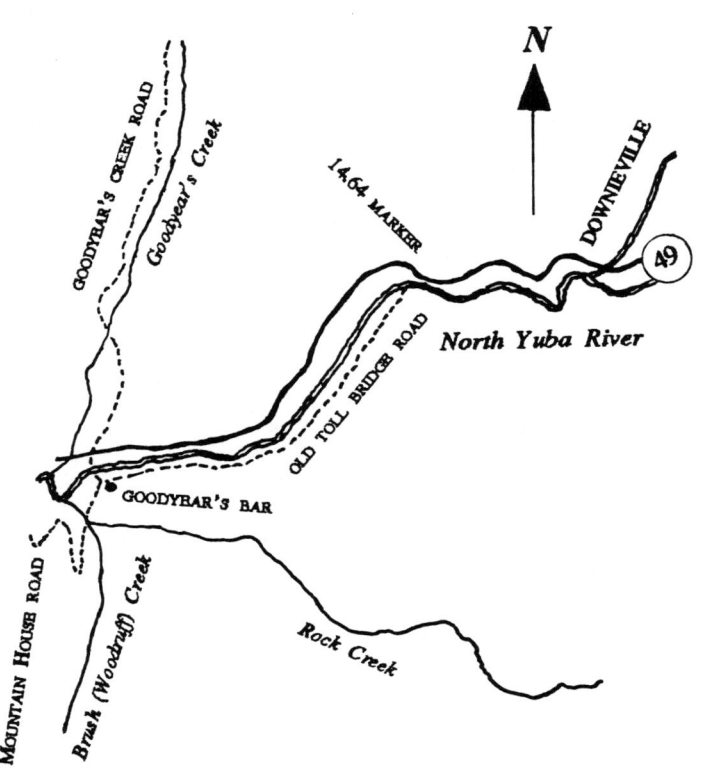

Goodyear's Bar to Downieville

GOODYEAR'S BAR TO DOWNIEVILLE

12.30--GOODYEAR'S BAR

Goodyear's Bar has a post office, some scattered dwellings, a decommissioned hotel, and a one-room school transformed into a community center. The Department of Fish and Game uses it as a planting site so that action near the single-lane iron bridge is periodically hot although not especially challenging. Kate Wolf, as some will remember, was a deservedly popular and gifted singer/song writer/musician (*Red-Tailed Hawk/Give Yourself to Love/Across the Great Divide*.) Kate grew up here, died much too young, and rests in the little cemetery near the community center. To reach the river, turn south at the Goodyear's Bar sign, cross the bridge, and turn east at the stop sign. This will put you on the Old Toll Bridge Road (Sierra County Route 402) that parallels the river for 1.8 miles. Access to the river at most points is easy--in fact this stretch is a launching point for river rafters during the early part of the season when the river is in spate. Here the North Yuba is is mainly wide, shallow, and full of boulders. It ought to provide good pocket water but has been only intermittently and stingily productive for me.

ROCK AND BRUSH CREEKS

To get to Rock Creek, turn right (west) at the stop sign where you'll pick up Sierra County Route 300, the Mountain House Road. Follow it .4 mile to the bridge over Rock Creek. You can park at wide spots at either end of the bridge and walk to the creek which is narrow, shallow, clear, rocky, steep, and brushy--in short, a real bear to fish. It holds small, native, and extremely shy fish including the occasional brookie. Walking this stream is demanding and the rewards may not be worth the effort.

Brush or Woodruff Creek is bridged a few hundred feet beyond Rock Creek. The road parallels it for just under half a mile. At that point the road hairpins away on its meandering trip to Forest and Alleghany. Brush Creek is smaller than Rock Creek and offers essentially the same conditions, that is, spooky fish and difficult conditions.

GOODYEAR'S CREEK

Goodyear's Creek feeds into the North Yuba from the north at the 12.20 marker. To get to it, turn north on Sierra County Route 400, the Goodyear's Creek Road. It bridges the creek about .5 mile from Highway 49. At this point the road becomes narrow, steep, and graveled--4x4 country. After the first stretch the stream is hard to reach and to fish.

14.64 MARKER--HIGHWAY 49

At this marker a seldom-used track closed by a locked pole gate leads to the river. The walk is short and not too steep. The north side of the river has seen extensive mining activity and dredgers continue to operate here during the summer. The river here is wide and offers a succession of riffles, pools, and low falls both up- and downstream from the point of access. Buzz Hackle, Renegade, and (less often) Elk Hair Caddis have been successful in this stretch which offers a good mile of attractive water.

16.70--DOWNSTREAM FROM THE FORKS

Proceed to Downieville. There is a parking lot opposite Downieville Motors at the town's western limit. Walk through the little park to the confluence of the North Yuba and the Downie--the Forks. I've never fished this stretch (too many people around) but there always seems to be an account circulating about how a nine year-old child took a four pound Brown out of here just last week. (Somebody else found a monster gold nugget at this spot not long ago. That triggered a real frenzy and ruined the fishing for a while.) I prefer to cross the bridge to the south side of the Yuba and then to fish downstream. This, too, is a beautiful stretch. At first there is a sort of levee with a path atop it set back a short distance from the river. At the base of the levee there is a wide shingle (or, in some spots, sand) beach along the slow-moving stream. The levee eventually gives out, the canyon narrows, and a rough track presents itself. Here the river divides with the north branch bearing the bulk of the flow. The branches come together to form a dream place--a short, fast riffle emptying into a long, deep, green pool. Flies with herl bodies seem to be effective here and in the stretch that follows, a succession of shallow rapids forming into pools. Dan at Downieville Motors said he took and released 30 fish in this stretch one recent Sunday morning. "I was using a fly," he said. Then he threw me a mocking grin. "I put a little piece of worm on the hook. That seemed to help." He didn't say what pattern he'd used; I didn't ask what kind of worm.

Rock Creek Near Goodyear's Bar

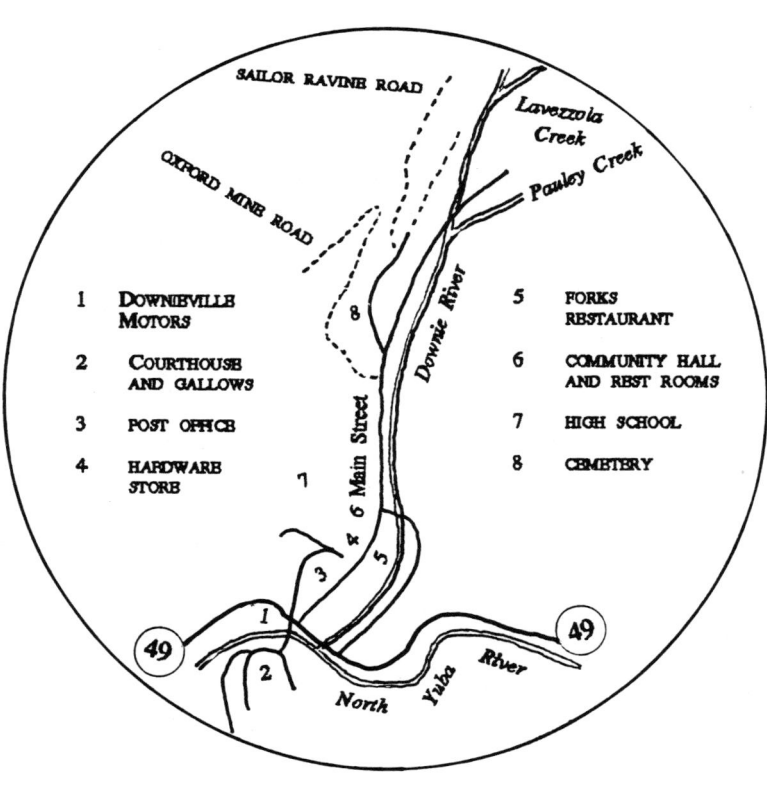

Downieville

ABOUT DOWNIEVILLE

Downieville, Sierra County's seat of government, is the hub when it comes to fishing the North Yuba watershed. Situated as it is, it is the gateway to the Downie river, Pauley and Lavezzola creeks, and the upper reaches of the North Yuba.

Back in 1852 the town claimed some 3,000 residents; today the population is a bit over 300. Then, gold mining was the name of the game; now, tourism is the life blood of the economy.

The Downieville Chamber of Commerce has prepared a useful walking tour map of Downieville that lists the facilities and services available in the community. Write them at P.O. Box 473, Downieville, CA 95936 to get a copy or pick up one almost anyplace in town. Try to resist the pull of the trout waters long enough to take a little time to get the feel of the place. Board sidewalks, verandaed old buildings fronting flush on the narrow main street, gas street lights, a museum, displays of artifacts of historic significance at the American Legion park, Masonic Hall, the County Courthouse, they're all worth a look. Across from the Courthouse stands a gallows, a replica of the one used once, in 1888, to carry out a badly bungled execution. (The story goes that the sheriff, reluctant to impose the sentence in the first place, in his agitation accidentally moved the lever that released the trap. The hangman who had not yet adjusted the noose and the victim plummeted through the trap but sustained no serious harm. They remounted the 13 steps to the platform and edgily took their places on the trapdoor whereupon events went from bad to worse. Those grisly details need not concern us here,)

Some of Downieville's points of interest are located on the map on the facing page. The town is named after Major William Downie who, it is said, in 1850 told the citizens he'd throw a panful of gold dust in the street if they named the settlement after him. (The story has an enchanting air of implausibility about it; nuggets, maybe but dust...? Hardly.)

There are four motels in the town, three restaurants, and an honest small town bakery that serves a no-frills lunch. The grocery store has a deli counter if you want to buy the makings for a picnic. The Legion park, more or less across the street and just above the confluence of the Downie and North Yuba rivers, has picnic tables.

To catch up on local happenings you can consult *The Mountain Messenger*, California's oldest weekly newspaper, which is published here. For somewhat less dependable accounts, the bench outside the

Downieville Grocery attracts the older male residents who swap stories and offer viewpoints and whose stock-in-trade is gilded (maybe gold-plated is more apt) nostalgia. They tolerate auditors. The other crowd, the young and restless, congregate evenings on the bench where Highway 49 and Main Street join. I think I know what they talk about but I'm past all that.

One great place to visit is the Sierra Hardware Store. Several reasons. First, this is an exemplary version of a nearly extinct species, a genuine hardware store that carries anything you might need to get along in what (in the outlying areas) is a harsh, unforgiving rural environment. Second, the store carries a good supply of fishing necessities including flies that work locally. Third, Tom Vilas, the proprietor, has been fly-fishing this area for fifty years and more. He doesn't get out very often nowadays but late last spring he went up to Lavezzola Creek and stopped counting after he'd taken and released fifty fish. "They were all small, though," he complained. "Some of them weren't any bigger than that," he said, spreading his thumb and forefinger maybe four inches. "They've got a nerve," he seemed to be saying. If you need directions, Tom can give them to you but you'll have to ask and what you get in reply may seem uselessly laconic. Listen good.

Cannon Point, a State Historic Site at the western edge of and overlooking the town is the final rusting place of an old iron cannon. They used to touch off the cannon to announce the arrival of the stage.

Ancient cannons and gallows to the contrary, Downieville is a slow-paced, quiet, comfortable place. I devoutly believe that how successful you are at fly-fishing is inextricably tied to your internal state. The ideal, I think, is one of calmness, serenity, and focus with all that other dreck submerged somewhere, not to return until you're back stuck in the gridlock. Downieville fosters growth of the attitude that allows you to accept flies snagged in tree branches, spills, missed rises, snarls in the line, too-light tippets snapped with contemptuous ease by a heavy fish, and long stretches of little or no action, while you are sustained, even exalted, by the pleasure of moving the line, the beauty of the surroundings, and the knowledge that you're hitting the right spots with a surgeon-like accuracy and skill. What more could you ask?

*The Forks -- the Confluence of the
North Yuba and Downie Rivers in Downieville*

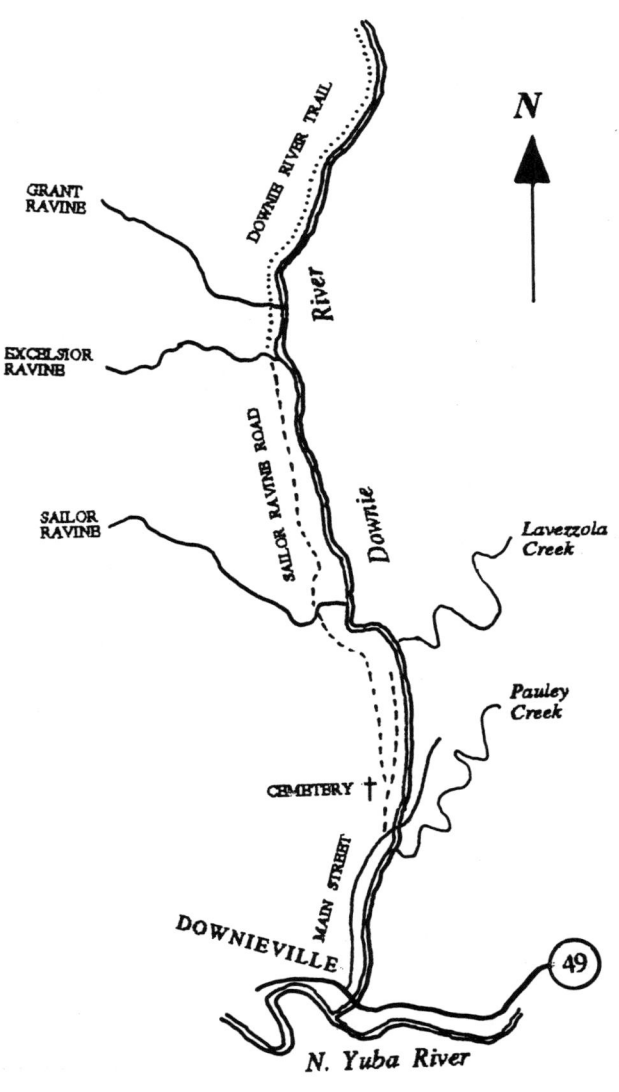

The Downie River

THE DOWNIE RIVER

You can fish the Downie River by picking it up where it empties into the North Yuba and tracing it upstream. The stream through here is shallow and relatively wide. The bulk of the town's dwellings perch on the sides of the river canyon so that you may draw an audience; you might even take a fish in this stretch but my slight experience with it has been disappointing.

I prefer to drive out Main Street, following it past Major Downie's home site to the point where Gold Bluff Road Ys off to the left. Don't let the "Not a Through Road" sign fake you out; you'll pass the cemetery at your left hand and, a bit farther on, the road will Y again with Sailor Ravine Road being the left fork and Gold Bluff Road continuing off to the right.

GOLD BLUFF ROAD

The paving on this fork soon gives way to gravel and not long after the gravel starts you'll come to a dead end defined by a locked gate. You can park there--the road is wide enough to offer a comfortable turnaround. If you were to go around the gate and walk the road you would quickly come to the site of the Gold Bluff Mine whose shaft yawns darkly at the base of the hill to the left. I usually walk directly to the river from where I park and am left with the choice of fishing up- or downstream. At this point the river is wide, shallow, and clear. I've only fished the downstream stretch a couple of times, mainly because it is not particularly inviting; there is little cover for fish and while it is open and easy to attack it hasn't provided a whole lot of action for me so I usually turn upstream. From the point of entry the wide, shallow conditions persist for a bit but you will soon come to a pool which lies below the mine site. The pool holds some larger fish including a few cagy browns. Once you've fished the pool you can get around it by pushing your way through the brush that lines the west bank and then re-entering the stream. Through here conditions are likely to be more favorable and may become quite good when you reach the pool at the point where Lavezzola debouches into the river. This spot is not only breath-takingly beautiful with Lavezzola cascading into the more tranquil Downie; it holds some large fish and is quite accessible.

After trying the Lavezzola/Downie confluence you can wade up the Downie. The flow diminishes markedly, maybe amounting to two-thirds of what it is after Lavezzola feeds into it. The river narrows a bit, swiftens, and becomes rocky with a succession of riffles and small pools. The trees in this stretch arch over the watercourse so that roll-casting is the name of the game (unless you enjoy getting hung up on tree branches.) This stretch is challenging and has yielded a good many fish.

THE RAVINE STRETCH

If you keep to the Sailor Ravine Road you'll be on a narrow, dusty, one-lane track that clings to the west side of the Downie canyon. (In dry weather you can manage the road in a 2-wheel drive vehicle with fairly good clearance--a pickup truck, for instance--but I'd stay off it in my Maserati.)

For the first couple of miles you'll be fairly high up the side of the canyon with no way of getting to the water. Press on and you'll pass an extensive dredging operation at streamside. Beyond this excrescence the road drops down and, at points, widens out so that you can park your vehicle and get to the river without having to be lowered on a rope.

You'll note that at any point along here you'll see tailings, mounds of boulders discarded by past (and present) generations of miners. (My friend, John Mumm, tells this story on his father who was severely bitten by the gold bug: a favorite place to look for gold is in the gravel under huge boulders. There was this house-sized boulder that the older Mumm believed shielded a fortune in nuggets and dust. He spent weeks tunneling under it and when he got to where he wanted to go he dug out his treasure trove--a rusted miner's pick.)

About five miles from town the road, such as it is, quits and the Downie River Trail picks up. From this point on the river narrows but offers a continually changing series of waters that hold fish--rainbows mostly, but browns as well. These fish are all natives so they need to be approached cautiously and quietly and the presentation of the fly has to be delicate and precise. At any promising site you seem to get one chance. The fish responds to the fly and either you connect or you don't. If you do, fine; bring in the fish if it stays on and then go on to the next promising spot. If you don't, go on to the next promising spot.

Along the Downie I've had my best luck with the Buzz Hackle or Renegade. Others report success with Gray Hackle Peacock or Elk Hair Caddis.

*The Confluence of the Downie River
and Lavezzola Creek*

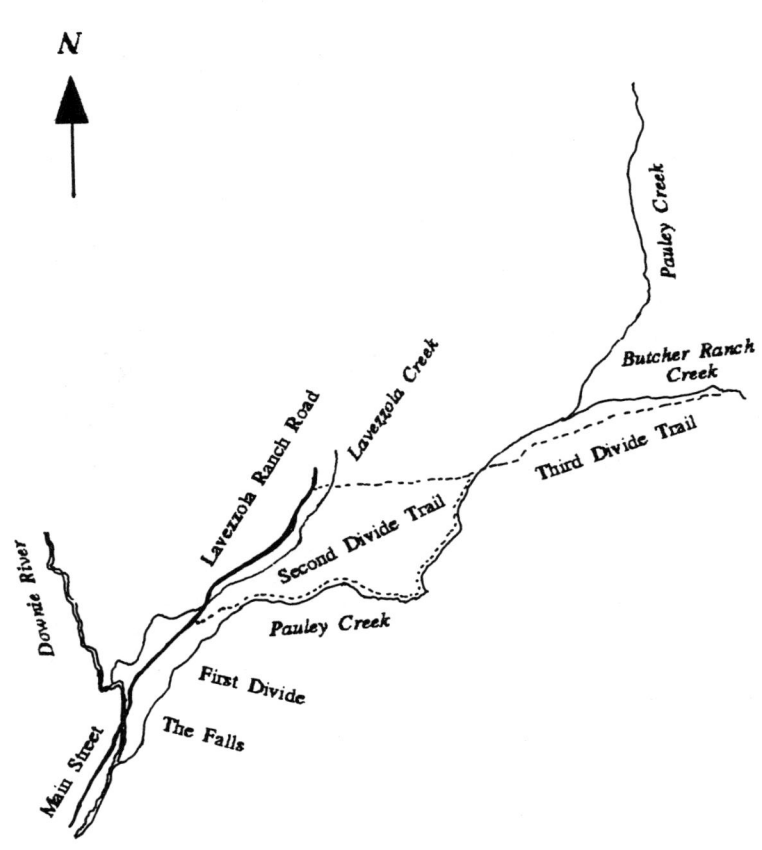

Pauley Creek

PAULEY CREEK

Of all the waters in the North Yuba drainage, I like Pauley Creek best. Why? From the pure (if somewhat myopic) standpoint of taking fish it doesn't outshine the other streams nor is it easier to work; it is not as accessible as some and it has more than its share of discomforts including clouds of pesky black flies during the hot weather.

The feelings toward a stretch of trout water originate close to the heart like those that gild the memory of a first car or a first love. Pauley is special, magical for me.

To get to Pauley, take Downieville's Main Street and head out of town. You'll quickly reach the Hospital Bridge, a new one-lane concrete affair over the Downie River. (The old iron structure it replaced stands a few yards upstream.) Pauley Creek merges with the Downie a stone's throw downstream from the bridge. Immediately past the bridge at your right you'll see the Downieville water treatment facility and a PG&E substation. You can get to the creek by parking by the water treatment plant and taking the signposted path to the falls.

PAULEY CREEK FALLS

Just a few hundred feet takes you to the falls (see the illustration, page 25), the gorgeous pool it has formed, and the water supply intake. From this point I've invariably fished upstream, ducking under the water pipes and scrambling down the bank to the stream above the falls. At this point the canyon is relatively broad and the stream ordinarily shallow and clear. For the first several hundred yards the stream is divided and the island that separates the branches supports considerable growth--chest-high Indian rhubarb whose delicate pink blossoms in early spring signal that the trout are ready to respond to flies, willows, and, in mid- or late summer, bright patches of pentstemon and goldenrod. The eastern channel has some nice riffles and pools that invariably hold fish.

Above the island the stream consists of a series of small pools with (in some instances) overhanging rocks or vegetation above undercut banks. Almost every pool will hold a resident fish and my experience, here as elsewhere, is that you get one chance. Because of the tyranny of the terrain, setting the hook is difficult so my scorecard along here reads about as follows: Number of rises = X; Number of hookups = $X/3$; Number of fish landed = $X/9$. The fish run small but they are all native and predominantly rainbows. One of the more melancholy images of this stretch that I carry around features the beefy, florid gent in Topsiders, black shorts a little too snug, white T-shirt, red gimme cap, who is drifting a glob of power bait molded onto a gold #6 treble hook over the falls and into the pool. I watched him for a long time, wondering.

FIRST DIVIDE

At the bridge Main Street becomes Lavezzola Ranch Road. It also becomes unpaved, narrow, and dusty. Logging has been going on above here for the past few years so there are logging trucks on the road and it pays to drive alertly and, when it comes to logging trucks, deferentially. On one-lane roads (which this one is, much of the time) the vehicle heading downhill has the right-of-way so, whenever a confrontation occurs the downhill vehicle backs until a wide spot turns up and the vehicles can edge past one another. When it comes to logging trucks I figure they've got the right-of-way no matter what.

The points of reference along here are the divides, ridges that have Pauley running at the base of the eastern slope with Lavezzola to the west. The First Divide isn't identified by a sign or marker, but it is easily spotted; at the crest of a long, easy grade you'll come to a spot with a high chain-link fence behind a cleared area at your left. A narrow lane angles back at the right hand. Park off the road, gear up, and walk the lane maybe a quarter of a mile, downhill, fairly gentle slope except for the last stretch where you'll probably leave the road and take a steep path to streamside. Along the way, depending on the time of year, you will see wild onion, mustard, ceanothus, monkey flower, and manzanita as well as the usual run of trees at this elevation including yellow pine, Douglas fir, several species of oak, and, near the water, alder and willows. This is a gorgeous stretch. Walking along the river is a bit challenging (lots of large rocks) but the stream is prototypical for the area, clear, sparkling water decending in a succession of swift riffles and pools. Along here you'll need to roll-cast. The always-dependable Buzz Hackle does the job hereabouts.

SECOND DIVIDE

The Second Divide is identified by a sign about 2.5 miles from town and there is a parking area right there. The Second Divide Trail

Pauley Creek -- The Falls

(11E33) takes off from the road and follows the crest in a roughly northeasterly direction. The trail is three to five hundred feet above the river which will be on your right and at the bottom of a steep, narrow canyon whose sides are too sheer (for me, at any rate) to negotiate. Stay on the trail and you'll come to a Y. The signs there declare that you've come two miles and the Third Divide Trail lies three miles ahead. (The good news is that I'm a compulsive step-counter and it takes me 1,800 steps from parking lot to Y so you will have actually covered only a bit more than a mile, so far.) Take the right fork. It drops steadily downhill and, after about 500 yards, it will bring you to an old, weathered miner's cabin at the edge of the creek. Above and below it are two splendid pools joined by a chute and a small waterfall. The pools are heavily fringed with Indian rhubarb.

The pools hold fish as do the waters both up- and downstream. The going is challenging with rock outcroppings that force the stream into a narrow, tumultous chute with huge boulders and downed trees to negotiate. You'll be doing some rock-climbing and plenty of roll-casting along here. Each stretch of wild water gives way to a crystal pool and each one seems to hold fish. In addition to the Buzz Hackle, Humpy and Renegade have served me well here.

If you are driven by restlessness or curiosity you can retrace to the Y and then take its other arm in the direction of the Third Divide Trail. At several points the trail drops down far enough so that you can get to the water easily. The conditions that you'll encounter mirror those I've described immediately above, that is, a narrow, fast-moving stream, somewhat demanding when it comes to technique, but immensely rewarding for its beauty, its challenge, and its productivity.

If you press on far enough you'll eventually intercept the Third Divide Train. Here, Butcher Ranch Creek enters Pauley. You can choose to continue on up Pauley (which becomes very narrow and brushy) or to follow the trail and try Butcher Ranch. However, Butcher Ranch can be approached from the east and, since it merits a place of its own, a later section of this book is devoted to it.

Pauley Creek

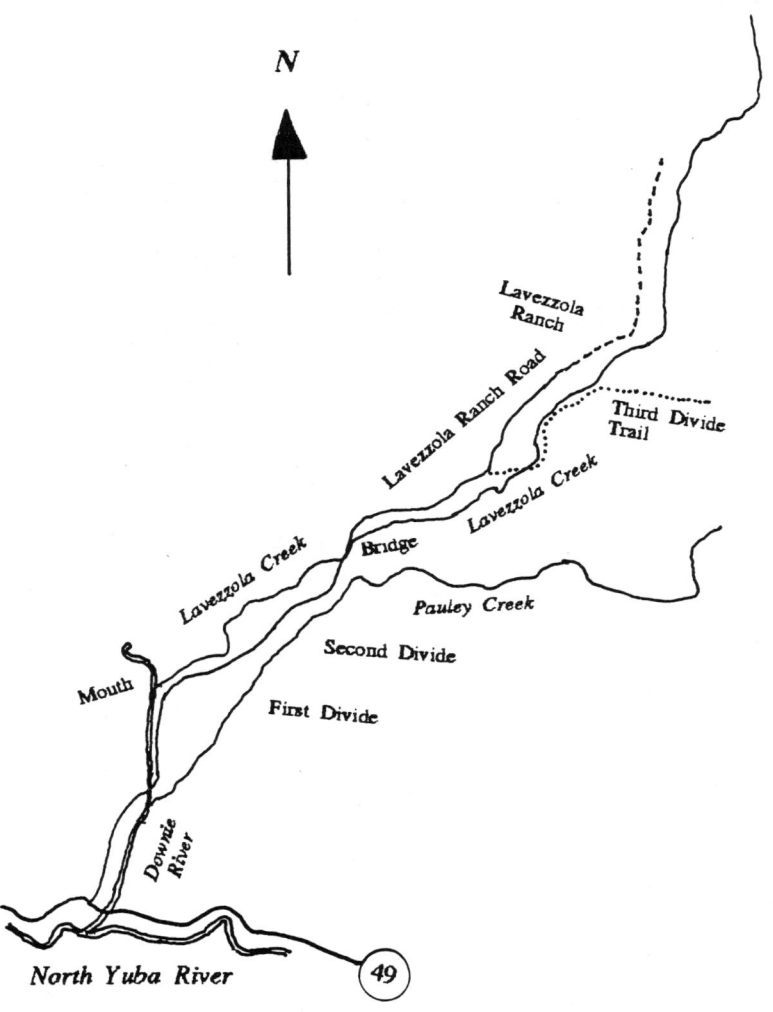

Lavezzola Creek

LAVEZZOLA CREEK

Lavezzola Creek has a glowing reputation among the small coterie of fly-fishermen who have had the opportunity to test it. Like all of the other streams in the area it has borne onslaughts by miners and loggers; there is scarcely a foot of the stream that doesn't show evidence of their activities. Even so, Lavezzola lends truth to Tennyson's declaration, *"For men may come and men may go/But I go on forever."* Beautiful as it is today, even with all the abuse it has endured and, somehow, weathered, one can't help experiencing a twinge of loss for what it must once have been.

The Gold Bluff Mine or Lavezzola Ranch roads (see the Downie River or Pauley Creek sections, preceding) will take you to the various access points to Lavezzola Creek.

THE MOUTH

As noted on page 19, Lavezzola cascades into the Downie River near the Gold Bluff Mine. There is a great pool there and the creek can be reached by fording the Downie above the confluence, walking around the brush and rock outcropping, and then proceeding upstream. This is a fairly tough assignment but when the conditions are right (late spring, after the heavy runoff has abated) this can be a lively stretch. There is considerable streamside vegetation so casting can be troublesome.

FIRST DIVIDE

At the First Divide (see page 24) walk around the chain-link fence on the west side of the Lavezzola Ranch Road and then follow the path that descends the Divide in a series of switchbacks. (Getting down is no problem, but the return trip will be fairly steep.) The stream here is narrow and brushy with a substantial amount of streamside growth, much like the section above the mouth. It is demanding without being particularly interesting.

THE BRIDGE

A short distance beyond the point where the Second Divide Trail meets Lavezzola Ranch Road the road will bridge Lavezzola Creek.

There is ample room to park and the downstream section can be reached from either side of the bridge. (During the summer there are usually a couple of dredges operating in the downstream stretch.) There is a wide, deep pool maybe five hundred feet downstream which has consistently held fish. Below the pool the going for the next mile or so becomes rocky and brushy with the stream tumbling along a fairly steep downhill course although there are occasional pools. The fish through here hold in the slack water behind rocks or boulders. The Elk Hair Caddis has been particularly effective hereabouts. Above the bridge the stream is wide and shallow but it narrows into a chute and pool just above the bridge. I usally walk to the center of the bridge and look for fish in the pool; if there are some to be seen I work the pool and then continue upstream. Here there are rapids and small pools that hold fish that seem especially responsive to Renegade and Buzz Hackle. The stream can be reached farther to the north at a couple of points if you don't mind a relatively hard scramble down fifty feet or so of steep bank that will take you to jewel-like spots.

THIRD DIVIDE TRAIL

Continue along the Lavezzola Ranch Road, enter the Empire Ranch property, and proceed to the designated parking area for the Third Divide Trail. Gear up and walk the short distance to the point where the trail takes off. A handsome foot bridge crosses Lavezzola Creek a few hundred feet from the trailhead. I've fished this stretch many times and in going over my notes (I've kept a detailed written record of every fishing visit to the North Yuba drainage) I find that I've taken fish along here under all sorts of conditions at all seasons of the year. Nymphs (Woolly Bugger, Pheasant Tail), flies (Humpy, Buzz Hackle, Renegade, Elk Hair Caddis) and my own version of a Ladybug have all worked. The nymphs are best in spring or fall; when using them I simply strip off line, let the nymph drift, and then retrieve slowly, either palming the line or reeling it in. Flies, on the other hand, are more likely to attract attention as they first touch the water or at the end of the drift, just before the current catches the line. There are a couple of miles of varied waters in this section and it is very easy to get to and to fish. I should also mention that Empire Creek enters the river just below the foot bridge and the pool it makes just below the culvert under the road (part of a failed hydroelectric power project) occasionally harbors some nice browns. Getting the fly to them is a bit tricky, though.

Lavezzola Creek Near the Third Divide

LAVEZZOLA RANCH

The public, county-maintained road ends at a locked gate at the boundary of the Lavezzola Ranch about a half-mile from the Third Divide and five miles from town. Park here and hike the private road to the stream--about one mile, uphill at first and then steeply downhill to its end. There will also be dredges working along here during the season. (On one occasion I stopped to chat with a couple of dredgers who were camped out along here with their neatly-coiffed miniature French poodle named, believe it or not, Fifi. Fifi made a lot of racket but, unlike most miners' dogs--and most miners keep dogs, big, surly ones--didn't represent much of a threat. They said there were lots of fish in the creek. I decided to fish a bit downstream from where they were working and, in that roily water, caught and released over a dozen fish inside of half an hour. I assumed they were stirring up a lot of food. I've had the same sort of experience on other occasions since then.) Through here are ideal stretches of holding water, riffles, and pools. The Buzz Hackle has never failed to attract fish all along here. Lavezzola Creek continues for a number of miles and a trail follows its course much of the way. The higher you go the smaller the stream (and the fish) become but, if you have the taste for a hike, try this stretch above the ranch. It supports a good many fish.

Tom Vilas bears out my observation that Lavezzola fish atypically tend to be most responsive during daytime hours and when the sun is on the water. I look for and often have good results at spots that are partly in sun and partly shade, wherever possible dropping the fly in on the sunny side and letting it drift to the shady section. Right at the line of demarcation, watch out.

Downieville Bridges

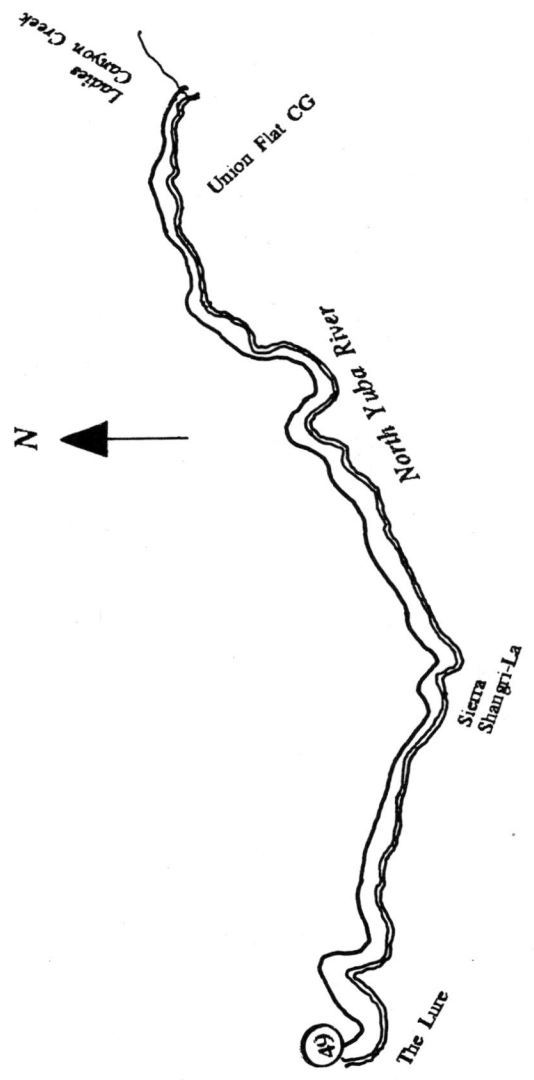

The North Yuba River: Downieville to Ladies Canyon Creek

DOWNIEVILLE TO LADIES CANYON CREEK

I confess that I haven't spent a lot of time fishing the seven miles of the North Yuba between the eastern limit of Downieville and Ladies Canyon Creek. The principal reason is that during this stretch the river and the highway are uncomfortably close together. I simply don't enjoy fishing in an environment where a logging truck or some other noisy and noisome diesel hauler slams by every few minutes. They make so much racket you can't even hear the fish.

Then, too, you're going to find that the human pressure along here is heavier than it is anywhere else on the river. The folks that lodge in Downieville town or at the two agreeable riverside hostels--The Lure and Sierra Shangri-La--or stay at the Union Flat Campground contribute swimmers, gold panners, and fisherpeople of all persuasions to the river. Combined with the dredgers who also work along here, this can be a busy place. And, there are also scattered dwellings on both sides of the stream that add to the load.

You will also note that east of Downieville the character of the river changes becoming smaller, narrower, and swifter. (The altitude, almost level fron Downieville west to the North Fork bridge, rises over 1,000 feet in the eleven miles that separate Downieville and its eastern neighbor, Sierra City.) You also see different vegetation; the lower elevation yellow pine and black oak begin to yield to live oak and Douglas fir although, come to think of it, that probably doesn't matter to the fish.

I have tried several spots along here, though, either in the evenings or early in the season when other waters were inaccessible or too high and turbulent to be fished.

17.70--THE LURE

Just a bit upstream from the bridge that takes you over the river to the housekeeping cabins offered by this facility you'll run into several spots where the river narrows and then opens into deep and inviting pools (inviting to spin fisherfolk and swimmers, too.) When conditions are right you'll have a hatch, an evening rise, and good dry fly conditions. One early spring evening when the water was very high and cold I hit a spot along here near the 19.40 marker. At this point the verge of the road had had concrete dribbled down it to prevent a washout. The river grumbles along a few feet below the road bed; in some respects it's an ugly and despoiled spot. The river veers away from the road and opens into a small pool. On the first cast (I was careless; a long and very slow day had spaced me out) a substantial fish took the fly. When I reacted too vigorously the tippet and fly went with the fish. That taught me one important and durable lesson; your first cast at any spot is the one most likely to draw a response --provided the cast is any good, of course--so pay particular attention to it. I regrouped and took and released four fish from that spot--none as big as the one that got away, of course, but nice.

19.60--SIERRA SHANGRI-LA

Just before the entrance to Sierra Shangri-La you will see one of the more dazzling spectacles the river affords. Here the entire flow is compressed into a narrow channel and bursts through two sheer rock abutments. Immediately above this point the river is shallow and rocky; the road ascends substantially above the level of the river and the gorge narrows. Then, at the 21.1 marker the road drops back close to the river and an interesting hole opens here. I've tried it a time or two to no effect; spin fishermen seem to gravitate to this place, maybe for good reason. The next short stretch is mainly shallow and aggressively rocky; I've never seen much reason to give it a try. However, after about a mile at the 22.0 marker you'll see a movable wooden bridge lying at streamside. Just upstream from it is a riffle and pool which has been kind to me on several occasions.

22.65--UNION FLAT CAMPGROUND

This campsite, carved out of mounds of tailings, lies right alongside the river. Access to the stream is extremely rocky and, just above the camp boundary the river divides with the main channel, narrow and turbulent, to the south. This spot attracts many gold panners; watch out for the holes they've dug. My records show that the few times I've worked these waters I've come away empty; worse, on one early spring day I got hung up on a streamside willow and lost the fly. Bad enough. Even worse, the tip of the lovely little cane rod I was using came out of its ferrule and was carried away by the high, rushing waters. Nothing I could do. I loved that rod made by some outfit nobody ever heard of in Denver. Just right. I did manage to fit a replacement but it has never been quite the same.

The North Yuba River East of Downieville

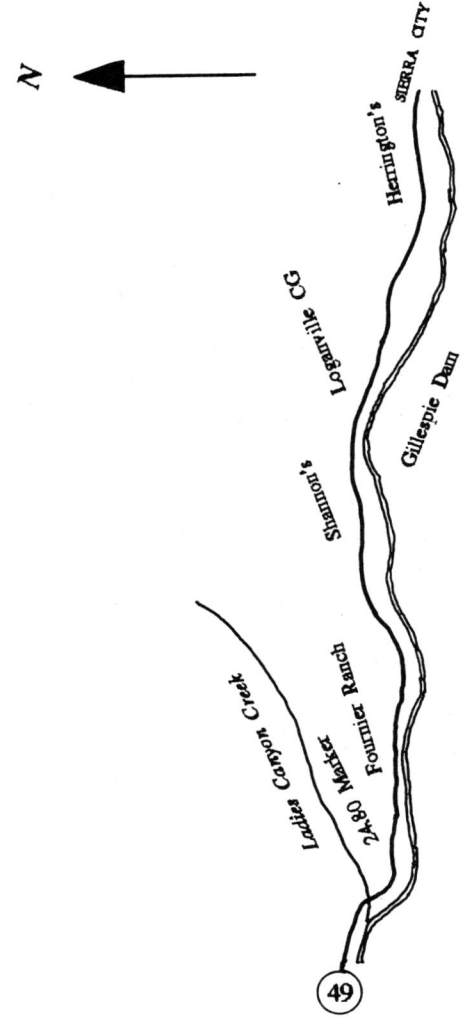

The North Yuba's "Trophy" Stretch
Ladies Canyon Creek to Sierra City

LADIES CANYON CREEK TO SIERRA CITY

My notes on what I choose to call the North Yuba's "Trophy" stretch--the four miles between Ladies Canyon Creek and Sierra City--take up a score of pages and thousands of words. Here's a bit of what they say.

Some years ago the California Department of Fish and Game set aside these waters as an experiment in native trout propogation. Anglers are limited to the use of a single barbless artificial lure and to keeping no more than two 10-inch or larger fish. The river is quite accessible along here and supports a substantial population of fish including a nice complement of larger ones. They are apt to be skittish and picky; on one occasion I noted that they would respond only to a size 16 Buzz Hackle. All other sizes and patterns, even in the 16 size, were totally ignored.

While there are numerous access points, the easier ones are:

24.80 MARKER

This spot is very close to the road. Here you have a riffle that forms into an elongated pool with a sheer rock wall defining the north bank. The pool flattens out into a short stretch of rapids and then empties into another pool with a rock wall, this time as its south bank. This pool, too, feeds into another riffle and then the river bends to the north and narrows into a deep, fast channel that hugs the roadside. The second pool is fringed with Indian rhubarb and has a dark and brooding quality. Usually you will see see dippers working the swift water and there are almost always *elegans*--aquatic garter snakes--writhing through the water to startle you. (The only rattlesnake I've ever encountered in this whole watershed was atop the northern rock wall here. It was small; not a keeper.)

I've taken fish throughout this entire stretch with Buzz Hackle and Humpy consistently doing well. By wading the stream you can easily cover the whole stretch from Ladies Canyon Creek to well past the Fournier Ranch. While access is easy the walking is taxing as the stream is hemmed in by rock walls at spots and holds ("holds," hell-- is made up of) boulders.

27.37--SHANNON'S CABINS

Park alongside the road at this spot and follow a rough road that will take you down to the river. There will be dredgers operating along here and, as a general rule, I try to avoid walking through miners' encampments since most of them harbor large and aggressive dogs. (Sierra county has a leash law which miners uniformly honor in the breach.) Once at streamside you will be in the middle of a couple of miles of absolutely gorgeous and extremely varied waters--riffles, chutes, pools, and, at Gillespie dam, a failed and arguably demented attempt to impound the river, a man-made waterfall. A spectacular whirlpool has formed below Gillespie's folly.

There is no part of this section that has not given up fish and the only counsel I can offer here is to try it out for yourself. The Elk Hair Caddis (and a Deer-Hair version of it) have been consistent winners along here. Smaller sizes, remember; 16 or 18.

27.70--LOGANVILLE CAMPGROUND

Take the western entrance to Loganville and drive through to Campsite 13. A short, steep trail will take you to the river--300 yards of switchbacks. The river here moves due west and offers the customary pattern of pools broken by shallow, swift, boulder-strewn rapids. During dredging season it is apt to be silty. You can walk the river downstream to Gillespie's dam or upstream all the way to the Sierra City boundary. You will find that at some points during low water the river is fordable and you will need to go from one side of the stream to the other to skirt the rock walls that periodically block streamside passage.

The most productive spots through here have consistently been the edges of white, fast water just where it enters the pools, in deep, shaded spots around large (VW Bug size or bigger) boulders, or along undercut banks, where they exist. Renegade has proven its worth here as well as the old reliable Buzz Hackle. I like to use Renegade when the light is failing because the white hackle makes it easier to follow.

This whole segment of the North Yuba is a joy to fish. The stream is fairly wide and there are few obstructions so that moving the line is conditioned only by the skill of the angler. However, I have noted that the action along here slows markedly about the time autumn sets in. The water becomes cruelly cold and the fish become lethargic and will respond only to the right pattern, perfectly presented. Best times here are June, after the initial snow-melt runoff has eased, until late August.

You can also get to this section by driving to Herrington's Sierra Pines Resort at Sierra City's western boundary, parking in their lush green parking lot, walking through the resort to the river, and fishing it downstream.

Finally, I am moved to remark that the rules about barbless artificial lures and limits that apply to this stretch are enforced, but laxly--not enough game wardens to do the job. As a result you'll probably see evidence of violators; empty salmon egg bottles, discarded snelled hook folders, tangles of 12-pound monofilament in the stream with a rusting treble hook at the end of a Mepps spinner snagged on a rock. When I encounter these malefactions the momentary rush of anger is salved by the satisfying realization that these culprits will inevitably roast in Hell's innermost circle. Justice, in these cases, while not swift, is certain.

NORTH FORK YUBA RIVER
EXPERIMENTAL TROUT MANAGEMENT AREA

THE NORTH FORK YUBA RIVER FROM LADIES CANYON CREEK UPSTREAM TO THE WESTERN BOUNDARY OF SIERRA CITY IS THE SITE OF AN EXPERIMENT TO IMPROVE FISHING

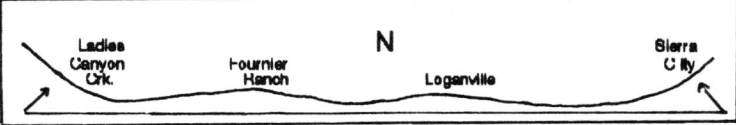

TO ENCOURAGE GROWTH AND PRODUCTION OF NATIVE TROUT
THIS AREA IS SUBJECT TO THE FOLLOWING ANGLING RESTRICTIONS

**LIMIT: 2 TROUT
MINIMUM SIZE FOR TROUT: 10 INCHES
METHOD OF TAKE FOR ALL FISH:
ARTIFICIAL LURES WITH SINGLE BARBLESS HOOKS
GOOD FISHING!**

SIERRA COUNTY FISH
AND GAME COMMISSION

STATE OF CALIFORNIA
RESOURCES AGENCIES
DEPT OF FISH AND GAME

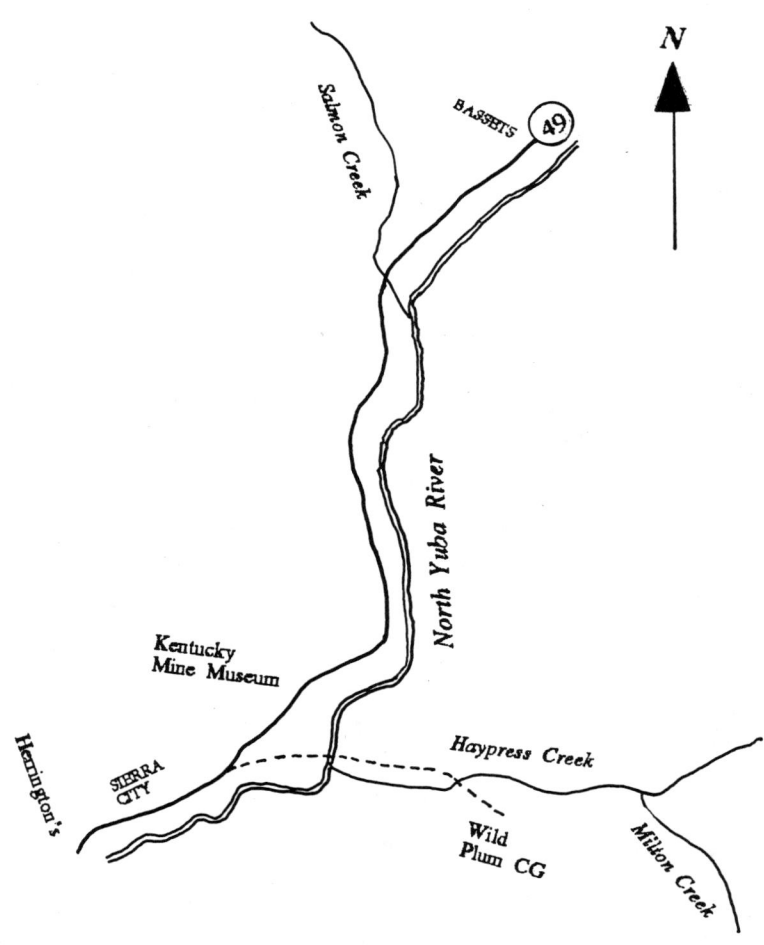

The North Yuba River--Sierra City to Bassetts

SIERRA CITY TO BASSETTS

28.80--HERRINGTON'S

Herrington's Sierra Pines Resort defines the eastern limit of the Trophy stretch of the North Yuba and the western boundary of Sierra City.

To reach the river at this point, park in Herrington's grassy parking lot that slopes up to the base of the looming Sierra Buttes and walk the road that wends behind the dining room down to the river. (Herrington's is an exemplary establishment. It offers comfortable and spacious motel units, an absolutely first-rate dining room, an agreeable bar, a gift shop, and a fish-for-a-fee trout pond that houses some sizable tenants.) Upstream from Herrington's the waters are seductive --riffles and pools that repeat themselves for nearly a mile to the confluence with Haypress Creek. Jimmy Austin who, at the age of 86, fly-fishes this stretch of the river (although he grudgingly admits to using hellgrammites in the spring) swears by the Gray Hackle Peacock through here; I like Buzz Hackle and Jerry favors Elk Hair Caddis. Downstream lie the Trophy waters whose virtues and limitations were discussed in the preceding section.

29.90--WILD PLUM ROAD

Wild Plum Road angles into Highway 49 at Sierra City's eastern limit. Take Wild Plum to the point where it bridges the North Yuba, park just past the bridge, and pick up the river. You will see that at this point the North Yuba becomes noticeably smaller (Haypress Creek which feeds into it just below the bridge contributes significantly to its flow) and much more turbulent. From this point to the river's source at the summit, a distance of about eleven miles, there is a 2,500 foot rise in altitude so the river is obliged to hurry along. I fished this stretch one late spring day in '92; it was a satisfying outing, considerable action and a goodly number of decent, lively fish, browns and 'bows, taken and let go. Late in the afternoon some ominous thunderheads rolled in and I managed to get back to the car just before the deluge hit. Sitting at the very top of a small fir tree across the road, not unlike a Christmas tree angel, was a Western Tanager whose vivid red head and blazing yellow body were highlighted by the dark clouds and the somber greenery. This was the highlight of what had already been a very good day.

30.22--KENTUCKY MINE MUSEUM

This has virtually nothing to do with fishing but the mine and museum are definitely worth a visit. Here are displayed interesting relics and mementos of a largely vanished past. The adjoining park has an outdoor amphitheater that stages a variety of entertainments during the summer months. The season's attractions will be well-publicized on placards that blanket the area and attending can be a lot of fun.

KENTUCKY MINE MUSEUM TO BASSETS

At the Kentucky Mine the river turns north and becomes narrower, shallower, and faster. You can reach it at any number of places through here and I've tried only a fraction of them. The results were mixed but I found that the going was demanding and the fish ran smaller than those in the stretch downstream. Moreover, it seemed to me that they were quicksilver-quick. You have to be very fast and even so you'll probably register a lot of misses.

Salmon Creek enters the river about a mile southwest of Bassetts and almost matches the amount of water that the river carries at that point, at least during the summer months. During the heavy spring runoff period the river is high and swift and the two or three times I've been here during high water have not been very successful. Dry flies didn't work at all and weighted nymphs at the end of a fast-sink line drew some attention and a lot of snags--about one bump to five snags as I recall.

Above Salmon Creek the North Yuba is a river in name only. Now it has become a fast-moving, shallow brook with the occasional small pool or other deeper spot holding the fish.

The six or so miles of river from Herrington's to Bassetts offers a smorgasbord of challenges. The terrain changes dramatically and the scale of everything diminishes; the size of the river, the trees, and even the fish shrinks. And, at Bassetts, with the abrupt, domineering Sierra Buttes now rising starkly to the west, even the fisherman suddenly feels dwarfed and humbled by the immensity, the grandeur and the rugged beauty of the surroundings. This is a place to be seen fully as much as to be fished.

The Sierra Buttes--Eastern Slope

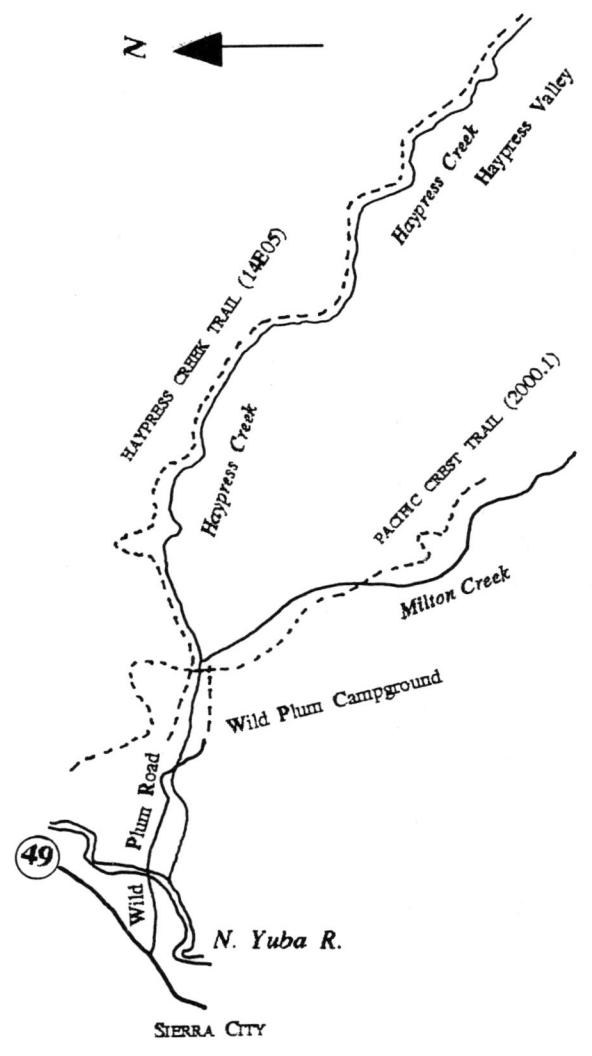

Haypress and Milton Creeks

HAYPRESS AND MILTON CREEKS

Haypress Creek joins the North Yuba at Sierra City's eastern edge. Wild Plum Road which branches off Highway 49 dead-ends in the Wild Plum campground which perches right alongside the creek. You can pick up the creek at the confluence and work it upstream as long as your legs hold out. I have had limited success with the first three-quarters of a mile of the creek during late spring and early fall.

The creek carries about one-third as much water as the North Yuba does; it flows in a generally northwesterly direction and is swift, shallow, and rocky with an occasional pool. Haypress has recently been turned to "productive" use by having some of its flow diverted to an electric power-generating station. The turbine is located alongside the creek just above the campground. Interestingly, the pool where the diverted water re-enters the stream always seems to hold a number of fish.

One of the nicest features of Wild Plum is that it gives access to a number of trails. There is a "loop" trail that offers an east, three-mile circuit of the campground. The loop trail connects with the Haypress Creek Trail (14E05) that parallels the creek the four miles up to the Haypress Valley and also intersects the Pacific Crest National Scenic Trail (2000.1) which roughly follows Milton Creek for a part of its long north-south journey. In addition, when the power plant was being constructed a road was built from the eastern boundary of the park to the diversion dam. The road is closed to vehicles now but I've taken this route to get to the section of the creek that lies above the power plant forebay. The walk is quite easy if you don't mind uphill; you ascend in the neighborhood of 800 feet in just under a mile. The creek through here holds a large population of smaller and extremely spooky fish.

I'm bound to admit that I haven't pushed on to the more remote stretches of Haypress. (I'm in the awkward position of not wanting to make the rigorous hike alone; my age-group peers justifiably fear the exertion, and the younger ones worry about me--or, maybe, carrying me out in the event of difficulties. However, the young bucks do say that it's a stiff walk with lots of action and virtually no competition once you get there.)

Milton Creek empties into Haypress a mile or so above the Wild Plum Campground. Insofar as Milton is concerned, I haven't tried it at all. Maybe next season.

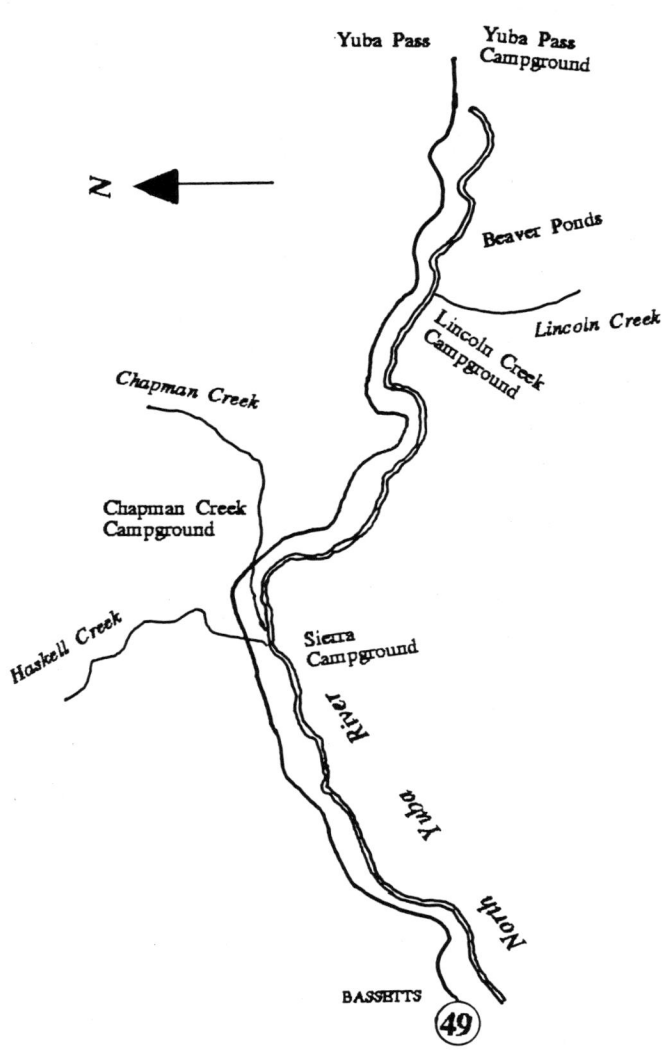

Bassetts to the Headwaters

BASSETTS TO THE HEADWATERS

From Bassetts to its headwaters the North Yuba is little more than a brook, shallow, fast, and brush-choked--at some points the streamside growth completely overarches the stream.

Despite the difficulties the terrain imposes these last six miles are well worth a try; there are fish to be had and the surroundings, especially in early summer, are breath-taking. The road closely follows the river which has curved to resume its westward course. At points small, lush meadows appear and the waist-high growth they support is a jumble of colors--yellows, whites, reds, blues of meadow goldenrod, yellow cinquefoil, yarrow milfoil, swamp onion, corn lily, fireweed, cow parsnip, western mountain aster, lupine. The river is easily accessible all through here and for much of it you'll see fish darting around. They'll be small and spooky and making an undetected approach will be difficult. Some fishermen take pride in recounting how, at times, they've crept or crawled to streamside in order to nail that canny lunker. So far I've managed to avoid going to that extreme. You won't have room for a back cast, you'll have lots of hang-ups, and at some points you may have to bend the rod bow-like to move the fly just a few feet. However, out of this test you get the feeling that you're in a decent contest where the odds favor the fish and that makes the activity somehow more meaningful--and precious. Consider. Anyone with a lot of money and no discernible skill can fly to some place where large fish can be hauled in until fatigue or *ennui* take over. For my money that's just not fishing.

40.22--THE BEAVER PONDS

The Beaver Ponds which lie just a mile west of the 6,701 foot summit of the Yuba Pass mark the headwaters of the North Yuba. Here are the notes I took on one visit to this spot one day in mid-June:

The beavers have built a series of dams in the shallow valley and the dams have caused ponds to form. The ponds aren't easy to fish because they are choked with downed trees--the casting has to be accurate to avoid snags and there is a lot of brush, willows mainly, to catch the back cast. The walk to this place is easy. The road is 200 feet or so above the valley. Park at the mileage sign and walk down the gentle slope to the first of the ponds. Pause to inspect--admire-- the beavers' handiwork. Dams made up of intricate weaves of small branches but the animals have felled and stripped some larger trees to get their materials. Some of the trees are nearly two feet in diameter and the fallers have worked to bring down the trees where they need to be. Phenomenal.

Walk to the first pond, approach it slowly and quietly. Fish are darting around the pond. I manage to take a half-dozen or so--all small and all but one of them browns.

It is fairly windy up here today and I have a certain amount of trouble casting but I manage to avoid most of the wrong kinds of hook-ups and I fish slowly and carefully. Move on to the next pond through the beaver-built debris and the masses of wild flowers. The going is fairly difficult because of the downed trees, the boggy conditions, and the near-invisible holes the beavers have excavated. I step in one of them and find myself hip-deep in icy water. Take a couple of fish, small ones again, out of the second pool, press on. That's the way it goes the rest of the afternoon. Get to a pond, first cast take a fish or lose it or have it miss the fly. Maybe take a half dozen fish in a pond, move on.

Eventually I work my way out of the beaver pond area--probably a three-quarter mile long stretch--and arrive at the stream itself. It meanders through flowery meadows and there are sheer cut banks and again fish to be seen and taken.

I lose count of the number of fish I release. Most of them small, in the 6-8 inch range. The largest one I land, all afternoon, is an 11-incher. They are about half and half browns and rainbows. All of them have been brought in with the Buzz Hackle. I try a variant spider but, interestingly, no action at all so I return to the Buzz Hackle which is immediately productive.

The temperature is dropping and it is getting quite dark even though it is only late afternoon. Earlier in the day it had been partly sunny with huge, billowing cumulus clouds. Now the clouds have gathered, lowered, and thickened and there is an occasional spit of rain. I continue fishing and the rain seems to trigger a feeding frenzy. Fish are now swarming to, fighting to get at the fly. On some casts I may have as many as four or five rises.

Thunder begins to roll and lightning starts to flash. I decide to return to the car and make the long, slow walk back. The rain gradually intensifies and the thunder and lightning are booming and crackling steadily as I trudge along. I arrive at the car just as the heavens open. The temperature drops abruptly, sheets of rain, hail, and even a few flakes of snow fall. That'll be it for today.

The North Yuba Near Its Source

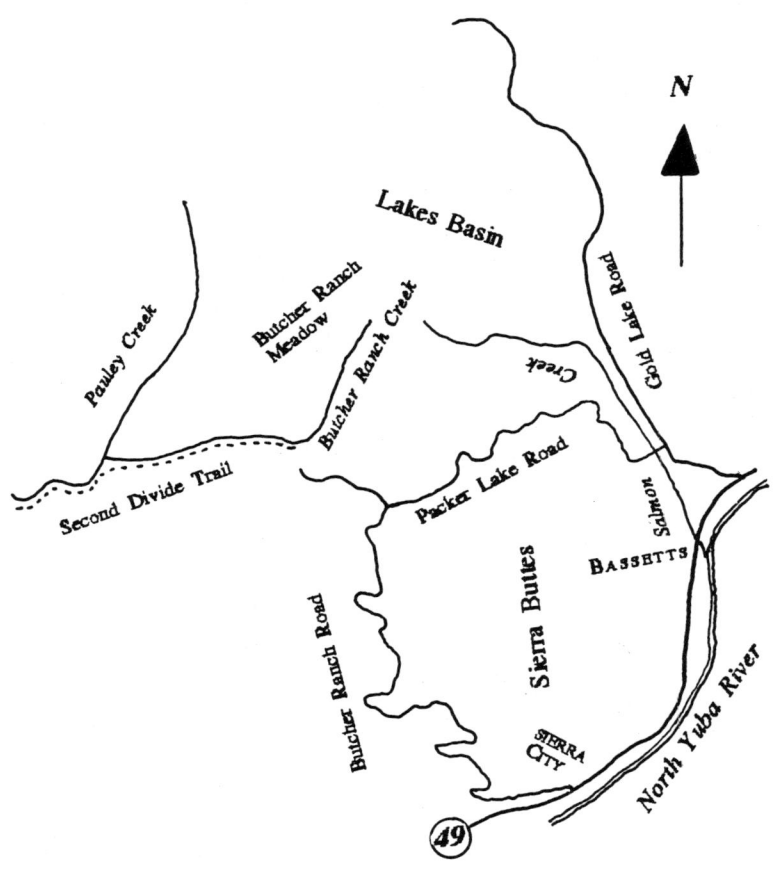

Salmon and Butcher Ranch Creeks and the Lakes Basin

SALMON AND BUTCHER RANCH CREEKS AND THE LAKES BASIN

32.90--SALMON CREEK

Salmon Creek empties into the North Yuba about a mile west of Bassetts. Its flow varies hugely with the seasons; in the spring it is a virtually unfishable torrent but it tames down to a fast-flowing, brawling brook in summer.

I've enjoyed fishing Salmon Creek. From its confluence with the North Yuba it ascends steeply, almost like a staircase, in a series of miniature falls and pools with each pool home to a fish or two. The going is a bit difficult, mainly because the stream bed is a devil's playground of giant-sized rocks and boulders. Walking along here is punishing work.

You can also access Salmon Creek by picking up the Gold Lakes Road at Bassetts and following it to the Sardine Lake Road turnoff. At that point the creek is at the edge of the Gold Lake Road and has been dammed just north of the point where Salmon Lake Road bridges it. The pool behind the dam and the stretch above it have been good to me on occasion and given up larger fish but they didn't have much spunk. Plants, probably.

BUTCHER RANCH CREEK

Getting to Butcher Ranch Creek entails some work. As we noted earlier, it can be approached from Downieville via the Second Divide Trail--a considerable walk. The alternative is to drive to Bassetts and the Gold Lakes Road to the Sardine Lake turnoff and then pick up Packer Lake Road. Just before reaching the Packer Lake Resort follow the left fork which will eventually put you on Butcher Ranch Road. If you have a 4-wheel drive vehicle you can get clear to the trailhead; if not, park along the road above Butcher Ranch Meadow and hike on through to the trail and, eventually, the creek. The walk in is downhill and easy but you'll feel it on the way back because of the altitude. Butcher Creek is small, brushy, and very demanding, not unlike the upper reaches of the North Yuba. However, the sub-Alpine surroundings are different--and gorgeous. Moreover, in addition to other species of trout it also supports a population of brookies. If you don't mind trying conditions and some serious work to get to them, Butcher Ranch is well worth a visit. Buzz Hackle has consistently worked on both Salmon and Butcher Ranch Creeks.

THE LAKES BASIN

The accompanying map doesn't represent the lakes that dot this area. There are literally scores of them, too many even to list in the space available. Nor have I fished them seriously. I have thrown flies from the shores of four or five of them on occasions when I was scouting around or happened to be staying at one of the rustic lodges that abound in the area but the bottom line is that I don't do lake fishing. (The few times I have made a half-hearted effort from lakeside haven't been barn-burners--I've taken a few fish but the more usual pattern is to come away empty-handed. And, I don't fish from a boat. I tried that once, in 1937, found it immensely boring and uncomfortable, and have never been presented with any argument persuasive enough to cause me to examine, much less rescind, that verdict.)

On the other hand, Dave Price fishes from a boat. Dave is going on ninety-two; he drives a GMC pickup with over 500,000 miles on it that carries a vanity plate that celebrates the year of his birth, 1901. Dave lives in Sierra City. He has spent a lot of time fishing the lakes, taken thousands of fish, and has the photographs to prove it. He has also invented "Dave's Special," a complicated arrangement of copper flashers that he declares to be infallible. Here, somewhat abridged, are his instructions to boat fishermen.

1. Troll very slowly--one and one-half m.p.h.
2. Let approximately 80 feet of line out SLOWLY.
3. Don't jerk the line on the first strike.
4. Set the hook on the second or third strike.

Best results are obtained during early morning Major solunar periods that last about two hours.

Dave concludes by saying, with the assurance born of long experience, "I have proven the above many times." Take his word for it; he has.

*The Lakes Basin near Upper Sardine Lake
in Early Spring*

HAZARDS

I don't mean to be a killjoy but there are a number of potential risks you should know about when fly-fishing the North Yuba.

Falls are probably the most common cause of injury. Wear footgear that will provide good traction and at least reduce the risk of taking a tumble. In my experience, felt-soled wading shoes or waders are the best all-around answer; if your sense of balance is somewhat uncertain, a rubber-tipped wading staff will give you a useful third leg.

You'll get thirsty while out there flailing the waters. Don't drink any stream water no matter how clear and inviting it appears to be. All of the watercourses carry *giardia*, a parasite that can cause acute gastric discomfort.

Be on the lookout for certain forms of harmful plants. The ones I have in mind are poison oak which is quite common in the lower elevations and blackberry tangles that like the moist areas near streamside. Contact with poison oak's oily juice triggers an extremely itchy rash in persons sensitive to it. (Depending on the frequency of previous contact, up to half of all individuals may react to poison oak.) Learn to recognize the plant with its three-parted leaflets, either low-growing or vine-like, and stay away from it. If you happen to come in contact with it, wash the exposed area with soap as soon as possible after exposure and apply any of several anti-pruritic medications that can be secured from your pharmacist.

Blackberries won't make you itch but blundering into a thicket of them can produce a lot of scratches and some serious discomfort. Everyone knows what blackberries look like; walk around them.

The mos dangerous hazard (especially to those who are allergic to *hymenoptera*--bee, hornet, wasp--stings) is posed by the common yellow jacket. Popularly referred to as meat bees, these ground nesters will attack in force if their nest is invaded. (I accidentally stepped on one of their dwellings last year; before I could get out of their range I had received fifteen painful stings.)

Other dangerous insects are *triatoma* (kissing bug), deer ticks, and fleas. The kissing bug, a dark brown or black, elongated, blood-sucking beetle can cause a severe reaction in people sensitive to it. It will likely invade your sleeping quarters and is not ordinarily encountered in the daylight hours or at streamside.

The deer tick, a small (pinhead-sized) animal, has provoked a furor of concern because it is a carrier of Lyme disease. The disease is potentially serious and debilitating but its prevalence has been wildly exaggerated. You may pick up a tick or two, especially earlier in the fishing season and at lower elevations. More than likely this will be the ordinary brown tick which (rarely) transmits spotted fever. Infection from the bite is the most common aftermath. Avoid exposure by wearing a long-sleeved shirt and a head covering. If you discover a tick on your person apply kerosene or nail polish remover to the insect's body to evict it. If you pull it off, inspect closely to see that the head is not left behind and apply an antiseptic.

Often in mid or late summer some of the higher altitude campgrounds may be closed because of an outbreak of plague in ground squirrels or chipmunks. The disease is transmitted by fleas to both rodents and humans and a few cases of plague are reported each summer. If you encounter a dead animal, to be on the safe side don't handle it.

The most feared hazard to people venturing into this part of the world is surely the western rattlesnake. It is also one of the least likely harm-bringers. There is an off chance you might run into one of these fellows so it is well to keep your eyes on where your feet (or hands) are going. In the extremely improbable event that you are bitten, keep calm and quiet, hold the site of the bite below heart level, and, if feasible, immobilize the bitten area by splinting it loosely. Get to or have someone call a first-aid station (Forest Service or Fire Department) for help. Do not ingest alcohol; the use of a tourniquet is strongly discouraged by medical authorities.

Another source of apprehension is bears and you will probably encounter bear signs alongside the waters around Downieville. There are bears in the area but I've never encountered one nor have I heard of anyone being attacked by one. I did run into one fisherman a couple of summers ago who said he was deathly afraid of bears and showed me his insurance policy--a nickel-plated .22 caliber revolver with a 2-inch barrel he carried in a shoulder holster. To do any real damage he'd have to shove that popgun right down the animal's throat before pulling the trigger.

There are also mountain lions but they, too, don't represent a threat except to other quadrapeds.

Finally, the conditions are sometimes windy, especially in the late afternoon when hot air from the valley funnels up through the canyons. Wind can add up to trouble for fly-fishermen who may suddenly find a fly sunk in one part or another of the body. To reduce risk I always wear a hat, a long-sleeved shirt, and (because I need them anyway) glasses secured by an elastic band. I also throw barbless hooks--they come out a lot easier.

USEFUL FLY PATTERNS

For fly-tiers, here are dressings for the flies that have been named as being useful in the preceding sections. (If you are not a fly-tier, consider taking it up. It is totally diverting and, once you've got to the point that what you're building doesn't look like it was turned out by Godzilla, extremely satisfying. The activity has it all over watching presidential campaigns or anything else on TV--especially fishing shows.)

You'll notice that there are no traditional upright-wing dry flies like Mosquito, Gold-Ribbed Hare's Ear, Iron Blue Dun, Adams, and the like on the list. Tom Vilas first drew this anomaly to my attention. Don't ask us why; that's just the way it is.

I tie almost all flies on standard dry fly barbless hooks, sizes 14 to 22; 16 is the number I choose most often.

Buzz Hackle

This is the premier fly for the North Yuba drainage and it seems to work at any time of the year. Some days I don't even try another pattern. (I will venture other patterns if I'm doing exceptionally well or getting skunked.)

Tail:	Fibers from dyed red duck quill
Tag:	Flat silver tinsel
Hackle:	At the bend of the hook, grey grizzly
Body:	Peacock herl
Hackle:	At eye of the hook, brown cock hackle

Deer Hair Caddis

Tail:	None
Body:	Yellow wool
Ribbing:	Yellow hackle tied Palmer
Wing:	Deer body hair about two-thirds length of body, medium to full size depending on buoyancy required. Tie butts down so that ends are exposed and flare up slightly.

Elk Hair Caddis

A consistently useful pattern for summer and fall use. There are a number of variations. Tie like the Deer Hair Caddis but use brown cock hackle for ribbing, orange or green wool or dubbing for body, and light tan elk hair for wing.

Grey Hackle Peacock

Probably the easiest fly in the world to tie.

- Tail: Red hackle fibers or Golden Pheasant tippet strands
- Body: Peacock herl
- Hackle: Grey grizzly

Grey Hackle Yellow

Like the Grey Hackle Peacock except thin yellow floss body.

Humpy

Humpy (or Goofus Bug) has a number of versions. Here's the one I like. I use red silk to build it.

- Tail: Deer hair
- Body: Red silk
- Wing: Deer hair, tied in at bend of hook and bent back to the eye.
- Hackle: Brown cock hackle tied dry

Ladybug

This is an original creation that grew out of the observation that during the spring there were often huge swarms of Ladybugs to be seen alongside the streams and that the fish seemed to go for them.

- Tail: None
- Hackle: Yellow, Palmered, along the shank of the hook and cropped short
- Body: Take a clump of orange-dyed deer hair. Place a piece of black floss (3-4 strands) so that it divides the deer hair. Tie on the deer hair/floss arrangement to the bend of the hook with the butts facing away from the eye. Bring the deer hair and floss forward and tie it down at the eye. Whip finish the head and apply head cement to the whole construction. (The black floss simulates the wing separation on the insect.)

Pheasant Tail Nymph

Tie this pattern on a nymph hook and use orange silk. Weight the shank by winding lead wire in the thorax area.

- Tail: 2-3 pheasant tail fibers
- Rib: Fine copper wire
- Body: Pheasant tail fibers
- Thorax: Pheasant tail fibers

Tie copper wire and body fibers at the bend. Wind on body material and tie off. Wind on copper wire as ribbing. Tie in thorax material at middle of shank, twist together, pull forward, and tie off at eye. Thorax materials simulate the wing case.

Renegade

This, too, is a simple and highly productive fly in North Yuba territory.

- Tail: None
- Hackle: At bend of hook, red cock
- Body: Peacock herl
- Hackle: At eye, white

Woolly Bugger

This fly works best in the spring, perhaps because it imitates the hellgrammite in appearance and motion. It should be tied on a 3 or 4X streamer hook.

- Tail: Black marabou feather
- Body: Olive or dull green chenille
- Hackle: Grey grizzly, Palmered

CAMPGROUNDS, CAMPING AREAS AND DAY USE SITES

North Yuba River

4.60--Carlton Flat Camping AreaA
Undeveloped: Vault toilets

4.87--Fiddle Creek CampgroundA
13 campsites: Vault toilets

5.35--Indian Valley CampgroundB
17 campsites: Vault toilets

5.50--Rocky Point Camping AreaA
Undeveloped: Portable toilets

7.79--Convict Flat Picnic AreaA
3 picnic sites: Privy

10.78--Ramshorn CampgroundB
16 campsites: Vault toilets

10.78--Indian Rock Picnic SiteA
3 picnic sites: Vault toilets

22.65--Union Flat CampgroundB
14 campsites: Vault toilets

27.70--Loganville CampgrouindA
20 campsites: Vault toilets

29.90--Wild Plum CampgroundB
47 campsites: Vault toilets

36.55--Sierra CampgroundA
16 campsites: Vault toilets

37.40--Chapman Creek CampgroundA
29 campsites: Vault toilets

38.50--Lincoln Creek CampgroundA
9 campsites: Vault toilets

Yuba Pass CampgroundB
20 campsites: Vault toilets

Sierra Buttes--Gold Lakes Area

Sardine CampgroundB
29 campsites: Vault toilets

Salmon Creek CampgroundB
31 campsites: Vault toilets

Snag Lake CampgroundA
16 undesignated sites: Vault toilets

Packer Lake Picnic GroundA
3 sites: Vault toilets

Sand Pond Picnic GroundA
16 sites: Vault toilets

Berger CampgroundA
10 undesignated campsites: Vault toilets

Diablo Camping AreaA
Undesignated campsites: Vault Toilets

Packsaddle Camping AreaA
Undeveloped campsites: Vault toilets

***

A following facility name indicates stream or river water source; purify before use
B following facility name indicates piped water supply

LODGINGS AND RESTAURANTS

Lodgings

Bassetts Station Motel
Hwy 49 and Gold Lake Rd.
Bassetts Station
862-1297

Busch & Herringlake Inn
Sierra City
862-1501

Buttes Motel
Sierra City
862-1179

Coyoteville Cabins
Highway 49
W. of Downieville
289-3624

Crandell's Riverside Motel
Commercial St.
Downieville
289-3574

Downieville Motor Inn
Downieville
289-3234

Saundra Dyer's Resort
Downieville
289-3308

Herrington's Sierra Pines Resort
Highway 49
Sierra City
862-1151

High Country Inn B&B
Sierra City
862-1530

The Lure Resort
Hwy 49
E. of Downieville

Robinson's Motel
Commercial St.
Downieville
289-3753

Shannon's Cabins
Hwy 49
W. of Sierra City
862-1287

Sierra Buttes Inn
Sierra City
862-1300

Sierra Chalet Motel
Sierra City
862-1110

Sierra Shangri-La
Hwy 49
E. of Downieville
289-3455

Note: All telephone numbers are in the 916 area code.

Restaurants

Bassett Station Cafe
Hwy 49 & Gold Lake Rd.
Bassetts
862-1297

Buckhorn Lodge
Hwy 49
Sierra City
862-1171

Cirino's at the Forks
Main St.
Downieville
1-800-540-2099

Coyoteville Diner
Hwy 49
.8 mi. west of Downieville
289-3624

Downieville Bakery
Hwy 49
Downieville
289-3674

Downieville Diner
Main St.
Downieville
289-3616

Herrington's Sierra Pines Resort
Hwy 49
Sierra City
862-1151

Indian Valley Outpost
Hwy 49
12 miles west of Downieville
289-3630

Mountain Shadows
Hwy 49
Sierra City
862-1536

Riverview Pizzeria
Hwy 49
Downieville
289-3540

Sardine Lake Resort
Upper Sardine Lake
Off Gold Lake Road
862-1196

Sierra Buttes Inn
Hwy 49
Sierra City
862-1300

****

All telephone numbers are in the 916 area code.

If you want to go a bit far afield from the North Yuba territory, the Mayo in Camptonville (288-3237) comes well-recommended.

ABOUT MINERS

I've encountered more miners than fishermen on the North Yuba. Generally miners are an agreeable and interesting lot who stand ready to respect fishermen's rights which include free passage along the streams. They are also generous with advice.

Miners fall into four groups; the largest consists of recreational gold-panners. For the most part these seekers are families--mom, dad, and kids or an older couple getting some rays, propelled by the faint hope of a bonanza. These folks almost never work established claims and are frequently seen scouring streams in or near campgrounds. They seem to be quite content with finding some color--a few grains, maybe a flake or two.

A second, technologically more advanced specie is the sniper. Snipers work in the stream, usually outfitted in a snorkel and a wet suit, and carrying a sharp-pointed hooked probe. The idea here is to find fissures in the rocky bed of the stream and to use the probe to tease out any bits of precious metal that may have found their way into the crevices. My friend Al Forney spends his summers sniping and says, "Well, I make wages...and better." How much better he doesn't say, even though pressed.

Dredgers work established claims. A dredge is nothing more than a powerful gasoline-powered suction device that picks up the gravel on the stream bed and pumps gravel and water into a sluice box where gravel, water, and gold, if any, are sorted out. Dredgers usually camp out on their claims. I try not to walk through their campsites, partly out of respect for their privacy and partly out of respect for their dogs. Dredgers are likely to tell you about the huge brown trout that lives in the hole just above where they are working.

Last of all there are a few large scale surface mining operations that entail the use of heavy equipment. I avoid these sites religiously.

All semi-serious miners that I've met hold four quirks in common: they are extremely close-mouthed about their success; each has a complex and passionately-held theory about where the gold is; each has an unshakable belief in the incomparable value of gold as a commodity; and each has a complicated system for playing the state Lotto. Most of their systems proceed from the belief that those numbered ping-pong balls obey something other than the laws of chance and are behaving according to a complex but knowable pattern that they are on the verge of discovering.

I've never met a wealthy miner; the guy who sells gold pans is doing fine.

NOTES

- -

INCREDIBLE FREE OFFER

Clip and return this coupon with a self-addressed, stamped envelope and receive, in return, one Buzz Hackle fly, the all-time, all-places best fly for North Yuba waters. Send to:

> The Salmo Press
> P.O. Box 329
> North San Juan, CA 95960

Offer expires on December 31, 1993

NOTES